Water Castle

Water Castle

Poems by

Natalie Solmer

© 2024 Natalie Solmer. All rights reserved.
This material may not be reproduced in any form, published,
reprinted, recorded, performed, broadcast,
rewritten, or redistributed without
the explicit permission of Natalie Solmer.
All such actions are strictly prohibited by law.

Cover image by Natalie Solmer
Author photo by C. Todd Fuqua

ISBN: 978-1-63980-645-4

Kelsay Books
502 South 1040 East, A-119
American Fork, Utah 84003
Kelsaybooks.com

This book is dedicated to my grandmothers:

Agnieszka Kalicki Kopec
&
Elfriede Nandzik Solmer Klockow

Acknowledgments

Many thanks to the editors of the following journals in which these poems first appeared, sometimes in slightly different form and/or with differing titles.

Anomaly Literary Journal: "Born Under a Lilac Bush"
Atticus Review: "Lilies Falling from the Ceiling"
Briar Cliff Review: "The Wind in from Chicago"
Colorado Review: "Am I the Saddest Person Ever to Stand on the Curve of The Earth, Or Is He?"
EcoTheo Review: "Girl of Water, I Could Swallow a Garden"
Glass: A Journal of Poetry: "Place the Lightning Bolt in Your Hair"
IUPUI, Religion, Spirituality and the Arts Online Exhibit: "A City on the Edge of Your Border"
Lit Literary Collective 'zine: "The Two Grandmothers"
The Literary Review and *Verse Daily:* "O Fortune, Are You Listening?"
Little Eagle Creek Anthology: "Where I Have Been All These Years"
The Louisville Review: "It Was Mango Season"
The Meadow: "Water Castle No.1"
Mom Egg Review: "I Am a Great Lake"
Notre Dame Review: "Stairwell into the Drum of the Earth," "The Psychic Medium Saw Lots of Horses"
Pirene's Fountain: "How I've Been Described"
Pleiades: "Girls of Lake"
Puerto Del Sol: "Dreaming with Virus, I Turn in Bed"
Rattle: "What Did We Do to Each Other in Our Past Lives?"

Contents

I. Snowbelt Wind

Water Castle No. 1	15
How I've Been Described	16
Because of a Riverbend Dancehall I Was Born	18
Saint Jude	20
To Reach Heaven's Bland, White Days	22
The Air Turns Soft & Thick When I'm Listening	24
A City on The Edge of Your Border	26
Girls of Lake	33
Place the Lightning Bolt in Your Hair	35
Am I the Saddest Person Ever to Stand on the Curve of the Earth, or Is He?	37
Quiz: Find Your Face Shape	40

II. Motherland

Water Castle No. 2	45
I Am a Great Lake	47
Dear Mother of My Mother's	49
The Wind in from Chicago	50
Girl of Water, I Could Swallow a Garden	52
Agnieszka	54
Dreaming, with Virus, I Turn in Bed	55
The Psychic Medium Saw Lots of Horses	56
Happy the World Could Blur	58
The Two Grandmothers	60
Born Under a Lilac Bush	63

III. Map in My Palm

Water Castle No. 3	71
Stairwell into the Drum of the Earth	73
O Fortune, Are You Listening?	76
Lilies Falling from the Ceiling	78
What Did We Do to Each Other in Our Past Lives?	80
Strollers in My Throat	82
It Was Mango Season	83
Everything Is Separated by Water	85
Boy Formed by Heat	86
When You Tell Me to Close the Gap in Our Youngest Son's Teeth, I Say No	88
Montego Bay	90
All Inclusive Resort	92
Black River	94
The Lovers	96
Where I Have Been All These Years	97
I Learned Love Late	99

I. Snowbelt Wind

Water Castle   No. 1

Consider, with me, my moats:
my double water body.

I merge & become all lake.
I swallow myself, the castle, the houses.

I flood the men, the sons.
Suck up your waters, they say,
No time for daughters.

Imaginary daughters disappearing
as I approach middle-age,
suddenly my body overflows.

Finally allowed land. For I have
rented my rooms, rented my bathtubs

in these complexes, these wannabe
castles, their lakes machine-dug:

ponds shining green at me,
reflecting raggedy lawn & willows.

Every castle was a glasshouse.
Now the mirror turns me into
Great Auntie. Now I sleep

in a house of brick and eat
a spoonful of the soil it sits on,
flowers everywhere.

How I've Been Described

I can see it in your face
somewhere across water

tell me which name
your lake-face

that *rises & falls*
with the cold, with bread

Moon-*wide cheek-boned*
Crab-heart trying to fill

straw-haired quiet
What's with the flowers

flowers, everywhere
so *folk*-minded

Cow-eyed
Horse-*legged*

Bow-thighed
Hilly forest *body*

Milk-*breasted*
Belly of the world

You, standing on those wide feet
what's the air like up there?

Oh, *tomboy*ish worm digger
Papery *seed collector*

Full of panic sky *disorder*
Hothouse orchid brain

Your singing mouth
full of wet felt

Because of a Riverbend Dancehall I Was Born

into the city which became famous for dying
city in which I grew among its acres
of broken factory windows & cathedrals
my parents meeting in the bend of the river

city in which I grew among its grandparents
gone, but I still search for the light in their kitchens
my parents, first generation kids, the river
their square, American dreams, singing Green-Eyed Lady

gone, but I still listen for the laughing in their kitchens
born of the mint fields just outside town
their square, American dreams sent down the highway
chopped and gone to Wrigley's, Chicago

I was born of the mint fields just outside town
my soul, menthol mixed with heady corn stench
what was chopped & sent to Chicago
from the mint fields, the ethanol plant rises like a palace

my soul, heady with corn stench, the grandparents
covered in lights at night—a palace, I used to think
from the mint fields the ethanol plant rises like a castle
I was told we were royalty from the old country

covered in lights at night—a palace, a lie
but don't ask any questions, don't ever go back
to the old country   My grandpa would tell a joke
about royalty   Listening quietly was my nature

I didn't ask questions   I just go back
to stare at what   was supposed to be
royalty   listening quietly my only religion
I was there when they poured   the concrete

      I stared at what my soul was supposed to be
        the highway   that ran through us
   I was there when they poured   the grandparents
  I go to take pictures of their houses   with new, living
owners

     pictures of the highway   running through us
in the city which is now   famous for dying
    to take pictures of their houses   that are alive
are my insides   my factory of   broken cathedrals

Saint Jude

Warmer days, we recessed on the lawn
with giant things—five ancient trees—
their wormy masses of roots we circled 'round.

There was a lone boulder I liked to leap
from & the concrete sewer-pipe
kids hid in, or I jumped

high from the swings.
We didn't talk about reincarnation,
just Jesus, who hung bleeding

above our round faces
every week when we helped with the mass
in that stained-glass church connected

to our school. It was named for
the patron saint of desperate cases
and lost causes. Who among us

could have been a true believer
I wondered, when we'd laugh at the delicious
curse words we hurled high in the air

when no elder could hear us. *Shit!*
We played Euchre and dodgeball in between
confessing our sins, our desires brushed close

to the boys in Catholic school basement
dances, then the sleepover and the midnight
Bloody Mary in the mirror I wouldn't join in.

In winter, recessing on the concrete lot
we were a flock of girls on a ledge singing
Raspberry Beret beneath a steel crucifix.

Jesus, we were loud! Choirgirls singing Prince
songs into the gray, into the snowbelt wind.
O god, how I miss that loudness—

To Reach Heaven's Bland, White Days

As a girl, I thought, No—

      it couldn't be why we were born

I was always

walking the playground's perimeter

until I thought of other lives

I began to speak

      to make noise

      when the wind

from the Great Lake blew gravel

at my pale legs

      beneath Catholic plaid

We girls screamed

our screams landing

      in the branches of just-leafing trees

Do you know that first neon-green

of South Bend trees?

Do you know

        that particular scream?

The Air Turns Soft & Thick When I'm Listening

    in the hours that don't hour before sunrise
there is a cloud before the glowy page.

    O cloud, I am trying to pull the story out.

I am telling you the story of my life
    by my own hand.

    I hate you, O cloud,

you don't tell me how to tell it.

I get scraps. My face is a border
    made up of people born elsewhere.

      I look up the name of their homeland, its translation—
    wetland, river, mist

When they were still alive,
    when my legs hopped the windowsill

      and I sought to consume the night,
    sometimes the clouds came up on me—

a wet fog.
    I didn't even know the name of

the place they were born.
    I was living the better life

      drunk on my mother's rooftop, half wanting to die

to leave the swampy land of my first love.
      I fled & loved a mountain range boy instead

      & I was poor & worked the land
      just like our ghosts.

A City on The Edge of Your Border

This Terrible Place

I wanted to be a cloud and forget my people.

I left home and the place of my father's father's
misdeeds, but the wind turned me around,

blew me down from the Blue Mountains, back
north to the place of the Great Lake hanging

over my body, until my body turned
into lake, into river.

O Waters,
the man didn't speak,
he struck

to get us out
to get the water out,
O waters of strife.

My father's father's father

he led us to this city as a promise
but now he can't see it.

Our progeny, this land,
will my children's children drink of it?

You Rebels

The river is a river
of money; the water, we make

her body into god's money.

Our god currency: sick white history:
the trade, the steel, the people.

When we can gaze on the water
we will pay. We will buy a view
and chop, then dig. When we want

what we want for cheap, no matter
the water ruined, we pay, they pay,

our descendants. Why did I even

give life? I am out of control

of everything. The wind kicks up.

Water Gushed Out

I stare into her brown face, *O Mother of God,* the icon
I inherited from my maternal side, *preserve the gift*

of faith. Our Lady of Czestochowa, pray for us:
for myself, my family, and my country.

Most of my grandparents are from
Silesia, a place meaning wet land

but also a place of mountains, of coal.
They left the mines, the farms, the after-war.

They left Silesia, in all of Europe
known as terrible, its pollution.

They came to the new pollution
place of my birth

a promise of factory money
and water still to drink.

After war, women are known
to sing a Song of the Sea

after the Sea of Reeds, enemies,
their soldiers drowned.

O what a chorus still
they say we've drained

half of all wetlands; O destruction melody,
melody that rises, that gains energy as it goes.

And They Drank

Shushushushushshushshushshush

This river is my ancestor,
artery, the genetic code.

I curve & curve
Which river am I?

The Odra?
The St. Joseph?

What the Potawatomi first named
Senathëwen Zibé, *Mystery River*

how the water comes roaring south then beats
north again—O mystery—and empties

into the blue heart of the MiddleWest.
The answer to the mystery is a map

of our topography.
My mother's baby blue house at the edge

of the North/South continental divide—I always
wondered at the metal highway sign

when driving over borders often
for lakes, for liquor, for men.

Holy in the Sight Of

The summer river is green, a dark emerald
swallowing light. My father and I
paddled a turquoise canoe

over it, careful not to
swallow the St. Joe water

like everyone said, holy with bacteria.

In mid-life my father lived
out by its swamps;

in the city, we'd bicycle
to where he grew, to parking lots

where I'd later sing vodka drunk.
When I can't sleep, I study these

street maps lit up in my palm,
telling myself to stay alive

calculating how many miles (2.7)
from where my father's father died
in backyard cherry tree (his own hand

tied the knot) to the riverbank
where the dancehall stood,
inside which my genesis:

my mother and father dancing, meeting
their family homes (1.2) miles apart

before the marriage,
before the divorce.
Someone said

A society treats nature
the way it treats its women.

My grandmother was finally leaving
my grandfather when he did it. My father still
says he doesn't understand my mother.

Someone said, Flood the land then
with menstrual blood. Wait.

I keep pleading with my sons to listen
not just to their father, but to their mother also.

There is something of the one
whose name means bitterness

in all of us, the one who streamed water
into the desert. When she died,
all turned to dust, the same one

who turns our blood to children,
who grows a city, who stretches out
across this border, all borders,

in the sight of her holiness,
hush and listen.

Girls of Lake

for Diane Seuss

It seemed there were always tornadoes blowing through you
every day of my childhood when the storm warnings rolled over

the thick, gray glass of our television and if the sirens didn't sing
from behind the curtains my mother made, if there wasn't death
    and wind

in our own square of lawn beyond that cloth, then it seemed
they were always calling in Cass, your county over from mine,
    reporting a funnel

in Dowagiac or Edwardsburg. When I was a girl and didn't know
    you
when I had the legs of a colt and you were done being an orchid on
    the streets

of New York City, when you had returned in the time of your white
    dress
and your good legs to the basin of the lakes, of your birth, a
    thousand milkweed pods

opened their cotton and drifted. We knew the same water meadows
same cattails and loosestrifes. I dug them up and collected the
    clumped clay

into plastic pots for my own pond. We both grew on a flat horizon
of lake and girl and the stacks of sky hammering the sky into us

the sky entering us down to our ankles forever.
We will never get the lake out of our hair.

We grew like the poison vines along the north/south
continental divide. I straddled it when I drove and was driven

around town I went with boys across the line
to buy liquor on Sundays. I skirted your girlhood home.

I skirted your Moon Cemetery
and dipped my skin into Diamond, into Eagle

Lakes at night where I lit cigarettes and rejected marriage
proposals. You and I, all our piss and waste flowing

north into the bowl of the big one, Michigan.
You have shown up at the threshold

of my remembering, and now I am born
again, given permission to name this wet paradise.

Place the Lightning Bolt in Your Hair

I know you have been eating bitter apple blossoms
for 20 years and are tired.

Each time love comes and goes with a season,
you begin to think of death.

I say now: pluck the lightning
bolt from your cloud and use it to pin up your hair—

the braids you braid in anger now
for too long you have seen the blot
of your father's father's suicide
around you. You say under all anger
is hurt, and your heart is just an orchid
covered in snow.
                But I say you will die this way.

I say stop crying in the garden,
                and gather flowers in anger,
set them on your altar in anger. Light the candle
and watch it melt.

Remember your people once worshipped rocks and trees,
Remember how you craved the woodland
while the baby
         inside you sucked down
every bit of magic like nectar and stretched your belly?
You left campus, poverty at your heels,
your family not speaking to you—

woman who followed the smell of trees.
You were led to the green

goddess of underworld. She stood bare-breasted in flower beds.
You ran from what tried to kill you. You must continue to run,
your gray fleece open and flapping to take flight
from the street.
                Don't worry if your birthday falls
on old Kupala night. Throw your wreath into the river.

Ask the black stork to steal your crown
from the men.
                It might be best if you never marry.
You already know the secret—   ferns don't bloom

Am I the Saddest Person Ever to Stand on the Curve of the Earth, or Is He?

What is my father?
All my lovers say they see him
through my brain of glass.

See the golden hair of his boyhood
darken like mine darkened.
See his suicide father

still alive and pulling my father's hair
to make him play piano
or clarinet in the family band.

So much he doesn't say, yet
our mouths still move the same
weird way, lips pulling back,

his Germanic tinge of pronunciation.
A rope curls
in me—

his laughter closed mouthed,
his camera lens his mouthpiece,
his hand a map of the open-mouthed forest.

In his pockets, a litany of children,
we his dollar signs, the Nineteen Eighties,
Wednesdays in fast food joints,

our leftover french fries in his mouth
too much salt, pressure in his heart,
pressure in my heart.

I slipped on his rabbit fur-lined gloves
as a girl I found the swamp
behind him and my stepmother's home.

I held the camera alone and took
a picture of my eyes, wetland and trees
in the ditch behind me. I was trying

to stamp the memory of light into me.
He explains he is trying to get the perfect
shot. He once went to the desert

to do his magic work on satellites,
programming their giant cameras.
He babbled to me in their math language

constantly, another language
I grew comfortable hearing and not
understanding. But I liked us best as bicyclists

when he took me to the other side of town
where he was born, followed the river down,
down to the root of it—we rolled

over sidewalks broken and sooty.
He once told me why he didn't like sad
stories or songs: "I've seen too much."

When his lens narrows in on me,
am I the saddest person ever
to stand on the curve or the earth, or

is he?
Here are the bicycles. Here are the huge maples.
Here is a father. All of my lovers line up.

I say to them: I have loved you all because of him
and loved me much less. I say: Damn
those star-made paths in us; let's

forget the fathers.
No, I mean—forget
that we thought we could forget.

Quiz: Find Your Face Shape

oval? round? heart? square?
which river's curve does your hairline follow?

the shape will determine

> can you see it in the mirror?
> does it show up on radar?

your fate

the earth's mud-green blood
flows while you close your eyes & sleep

> make a cross across your face and measure:
> how many family secrets from brow to chin?

your face

compare the numbers, compare yourself
to these celebrity images:

> when *Seventeen* opined on the four types
> (this quiz determines your coif, your style,
> your fate & brow—what is the most
> attractive type?)

I failed, sullen in my weird outline.
I was thinking, *hexagon?*

> now my face has turned—I mean, my fate
> "experts have discovered" three more face shapes:
> rectangle, triangle, & "the most rare of all, *diamond*"

diamonds, diamonds, diamonds: the shape of your fate

      has an expert seen me?
      men saw me as odd or beautiful, not cute

<u>narrow forehead</u>:

      but the homeliness of middle age is freedom
when the men stopped asking where I'm from:
Sweden? Russia? Switzerland?

*(and to explain I'm born here, just looking like my ancestors
and why is no one thinking of Poland? Her name?)*

<u>Wide, dramatic cheekbones</u>:

      my face is as wide as the shovel
of my ancestors who sold vegetables &
soldiered in the wars of the empires

<u>Pointed chin</u>:

      when I was a teenager running
on the sidewalk & men howled at me
I spit at their feet

      diamond, diamond, diamond

I read about a starlet whose face was deemed
a diamond, but when I clicked on the next page

      she was no longer:
      the next set of experts judged her as square

I flip back and forth
image to image

the lens, the hours, the ultimate
morph. how much

      did she pay for plastic? how much

can we dent
the shape of our fate?

II. Motherland

Water Castle   No. 2

In his gold phase, Gustav Klimt stood in a rowboat
on Lake Attersee, staring at the *Schloss Kammer*,
painting for pleasure, for summer vacation, the famous Water
   Castle.

In the distance, the mountains named for Hell
and an easterly wind named for the scent of roses.

The castle changes empires and names, becomes a hotel.

Origin is unimportant—avoidance is
The thing recorded. My ancestor's mountains are mine as well.
Nancy Chen Long writes in Indiana.

When Klimt died in Vienna,
my paternal grandfather was 26 minutes away by train—

a child living just outside that city with his gray-eyed mother.
No one knows how she ended up there from Czech Silesia.

My sister & I visited Salzburg once,
so close to the Water Castle I didn't know of yet.

We passed a shop window displaying dirndls.
She joked we should buy one—isn't that our ancestry?

Could we buy it? Ancestry? That's as far east
as we went, still questioning a train to Poland.

When we asked our maternal grandfather
about visiting his birthplace, he told us,

Why in the hell would you wanna do that?
Don't go.

We were not allowed to ask him about the Old Country
or fathers. He came over with his mother, alone.

We were told she couldn't marry his father,
though they wanted to, because he was royalty.

I buy the ancestry test for my mother.
I have almost proved my knowing: her grandfather
was Jewish, not Polish nobility.

There it is: the small thing that passes
in the blood. I used to scoff at my ancestors

for coming to this Northern Indiana city of factories
that fell. How dare they enter at the green feet

of the Lady of this shore and catch a train
west? For decades, I wanted nothing of my bare root.

I fled lake & plain for blue & green mountains,
and at my tables in my rented rooms: beloved

friends from any place & tongue other than
my non-place, my unknown.

I Am a Great Lake

Everclear spilled, slicked
the table, its

decks of cards, phones didn't exist
in our pockets or hands

but Euchre. We learned it in school
playing in our plaid skirt uniforms.

My friend licked the liquor up.
All of us licked the liquor up

until I had to stop. Until alcohol
became old as me.

I am as old as the rusted out mini-van
we drove around in, blasting *The Score*.

I am old as the bats
that swarmed the summer evenings

around the baseball stadium lights, the empty
factory's brick façade behind them.

I am Studebaker's brick façade, old
as a summer evening

Smirnov in a 7-11 Slurpee,
my sandal thrown out the van's window

as we drove to the forbidden beach
up the highway to the Great Lake.

I am a Great Lake, so
old, girlfriends singing

no one knowing our location
as old as midnight

as sneaking in my mother's door
just in time

old enough now to become
my mother's door.

Dear Mother of My Mother's

mother's mother's . . .
It is rare for me to be alive

and have you as ancestor, they say.
When I open the map—

your living children are a dark stain
all around the Baltic,

most dense in Siberian wilderness,
and the Kalash of Pakistan.

By some miracle, some linked mitochondria, some ocean steamer,
I have been spit out here.

Your cradle the glacial
that filled in the ice all around me.

6,500 years ago, a bottleneck in Ukraine
where you longed for the colors of plant life.

You'd paint anything you could find
my mother's mother's

mother cut up the cardboard waste,
rinsed out glass bottles

for her canvas to paint, for her nerves
for the anticipation of cold or of violence.

Only the mothers know how easily
we are erased.

The Wind in from Chicago

followed the train track   east
howled through my youth   and howled
through my body   like my body was trellis

I was tall and rigid   needing
to be held   filled squares
with the tendrils

of what I grew   on our chain-link
the grape vine   honeysuckle   clematis
sweet pea   and trumpet vine

the wind in from Chicago
knocked over   lawn chairs in the yard
lifted my plaid   uniform skirt

I ran to gather my garden shovels
and felt the earth's   roll
sway me   like a bell

against the lake-sky
always the shadow   of water
a lake howling   in my hair

my mother's tea roses   howling
I petted them   the bumblebees
and cried   then opened

and closed   a sweet pea's mouth
purple-pink   I stuck my bare toes
into the silver links   and hopped over

into what wild lots   still left
once I took that train   west
at fifteen   and found out

the source   of the howling
empty   links and squares   this boy
in my hair   forever

Girl of Water, I Could Swallow a Garden

with my two ungloved hands
tear every undesirable by the root—
pile their light bodies neatly in the barrow.

I remember standing in a field of men at the botanical garden
holding my shining spade. I remember
what the frat boy doing community service
said to me when I told him to plant.

The sweet potato vines winced,
waved their purple leaves from small, black pots.

There is a photograph my father captured
when visiting: me roaming

those grounds I mulched & culled & greenhoused:
long-limbed slip of me,
doe-eyed by the ponds, a girl

full of yellowing waterlilies,
a green image left on paper.

My father has stopped photographing light,
misremembers my name, disappears me.

Now there are trees in that Carolina city
I planted that are twice, three times as tall
as my sons. Now I am so far from the red

dust and fire
ants that bit my skin every day.

People say I used to go around asking for smoke,
say I used to wander through the camellia collection
following boys who carried instruments.

I say I remember riding in the truck looking for coyote
on coffee breaks with Joey, I
remember the one true line I wrote
in those years of landscape and heat:

I'm really a poet. I'm just here for the snakes.

Agnieszka

You saw prophesy in loaves of bread, in crooked
picture frames and flocks of crows on the lawn.

In dreams you were given the accurate predictions
of fire and of funerals.

Your daughters speak of the one time
you could not get out of bed after confession.

Each daughter telling a different story
about where you went and for how long.

They say they knew I was like you. I think this why
your acceptance, love for me, unmatched.

When they lowered you into the soil,
it was the year of your fourth daughter

my mother, a bride again.
I turned to soil, ten years old

I bought garden seeds, ten cents each,
for the dead lawn of my changed landscape.

Everyone left in the dust blue house so scared for me—
how right and how wrong they all were.

Dreaming, with Virus, I Turn in Bed

startle to see you lying next to me, body half-covered
by a *pierzyna* like the ones
you tucked around my little body as a girl.

Now you are alive again as I never saw you,
not much older than a girl—my mother's face
flickering in your powdered face, your rose lips,

your cheekbones high and curved as apples,
and your brown hair roller-curled, resting on my pillows.

You smile with your sea-colored eyes into my fever—
I am dazzled, silent, so you pinch me above my breast

and wake me. My phone glows:
4:30am. I switch on the green lamp
to get your ghost out of my blankets.

The hours open a mourning dove sky
when I realize the date—

that number you were called back
from your white sheet sickbed and left
and I—

    I got lost.

Now I am back in my body cutting
the first roses of the season
in sacrifice.

I place your picture, the vase with water.

    I light the wicks.

The Psychic Medium Saw Lots of Horses

Franciszek working the onion fields and then
his message to me, Your sons! Look at the boys!

His great-grandsons. Something about if
we were working a farm, the farm of his boyhood.

When he was alive, he told me:
We had to speak German in the fields.

And then told me not to go back.
Don't ever go back

to the land that so often erased its name
of its people, our people.

I was twenty-two and didn't think in terms of a 'people'
or any people. My mother said, No use going back.

All record of us surely destroyed.
I thought of Franciszek as the land and me

disappearing—a fragment, a dish, bones in my face,
a golden icon hanging from a thin nail—cheap and common.

He told me, Never romanticize it.
After I read to him the ballad of his life

I wrote as assignment in college—my big idea,
my big chance to ask the questions

his own daughters were too afraid to ask.
But he joked and swerved from their territory.

I never asked, and even though he warned against
romanticism, as I read him the poem,

his eyes turned green and wet.
He is the one who gave the family this city

and eyes that change color.
Here. Here's where it happened—

the factory he rose in,
remembering horses.

Happy the World Could Blur

the glass around me could evaporate, when taking shots
from little paper cups in our parents' bathrooms.

I was jumping in a kitchen, ecstatic:
I don't know where I am! I don't know where I am!

It was my mother's kitchen.
I never knew it was so yellow.

I was finally warm.
Finally, I was talking

in the world with the other girls.
Vodka was the world.

We bought alcohol on the Westside
until a bullet came for the man

who sold to us. We kept going
to that one house—

St. Ides and boys with
drums & guitar
until the bullets came this time

for that house and I had no sense
spinning a boy 'round and 'round
on the gravel drive, I made him

sick, never knew
the map in me
until I was old, colder

sober, touching the skin of my phone
again & again to enlarge the streets

of my youth when I can't sleep & then
I see my grandpa slept one street away

while I spun drunk, so close. Now I can only see him
in dreams. In dreams I cry while he sings & sings.

The Two Grandmothers

In their afterlife   some days I see them
sitting side by side like the Two Fridas
quiet with each other   they face my strange

life   and just when I think I'll paint
tears falling from their faces   Elfriede
lights up a cigar   adjusts her cleavage

in her satin blouse   clicks her boot-heels
Agnieszka waves away Elfriede's smoke   clutches
her necklace   a small blue Mary medallion

she slides back and forth   over the chain
Agnieszka   aside to me   *Can you put me back
in my pink kitchen now?*   Her light blue eyes

are still all light   She never worked   drove
after she had her five kids   *What?   I was
a seamstress, baker cook! Don't forget! I worked!*

Her eyes   Saint Saint   I think every goodness
in me must come from her   *Psh!*   She waves
my thoughts away   her wine-red heart still showing

over her flower-embroidered   white button-down
where I painted it   in my head   *And what's with
these blood-red veins anyway?   How they travel

outside us   and lead straight to you?*   Elfriede
complains   *These tethers are making me uncomfortable
This isn't working*   I allow Agnieszka to go back

to her midnights   her davenport   watching Carson
or Golden Girls   laughing in the dark   Elfriede says
It's bad enough you've cut away at our chests!

Why don't you just put us in our wedding dresses?
Or at least I'll wear my Russian fur hat   or put me
in the garden with my troll figurines   Give me

a beer   my German dolls   You always thought
I was a bad person because you heard me say
I don't like babies   You should understand

now that you've fantasized about leaving your own
infants   and their father has never struck you   So what
if I had a little German band   and I played trombone?

What music do you want from me? What use are we to you now
if you never listen?   You're so much like me you can't even
stand it   She smiles a sharp smile   now both grandmothers are
    speaking

so fast   I can't get all the words on the page   I let them loose
and take a break   In the bathroom   I try to find my bones
Whose lips?   Whose nose?   Whose poverty and sadness

in the gene?   The grandmothers have wandered back to where
they were sitting   but they've defected   stitched up their hearts
and put on their wedding gowns   the cords from their chests

that lead and pinch back into my own are nothing but ghostly
outline   transparent   white   They have turned themselves
young again   and are almost too beautiful to look at   They kid

each other   delight in their lithe bodies   and start to dance
a polka together   *We want to feel our skirts spinning!*   Each
one takes a turn laughing   trying to teach the other a style

a step *Yes Yes   We are here   What is it you want?*

Born Under a Lilac Bush

I.

In my mirror there's always grandmother,
the one with birds in her laundry.

She writes that fig tree in her small
California yard took up all the air

and brought those birds to her clothesline,
shitting and singing. When I wake up,

Elfriede hovers around my cheekbones,
Elfriede hovers around my mountain—

the floor pile of clean laundry I leave all week
and pluck my children's outfits out of.

II.

When I had courage once, I asked Elfriede
where she was born—*under a lilac bush*

on a mountain, for all I know. After her death,
my uncle sent me photographs of the village,

its faded *Pomorzowice* sign—black on white,
vandalized by someone who wrote *Victoria*

in a red like lipstick or blood. Around it,
the tall grass had gone to seed. Elfriede was

two years old when she left Upper Silesia for Indiana.
In her twenties, on the train leaving California

she cursed Indiana, her husband's crooked house
that waited there, she cursed her husband's wine

bottles, the time she slapped him for throwing
the cat, she cursed everything he did back,

pregnant with another son
on the train.

III.

Notes from her typewriter—
Compton, California 1945

Other immigrants, small house,
a lot of fields, husband, baby, stray cat.

When it rained, the high curbs filled
with water and even their shoes

turned green in the closet. Newspaper
curtains. One frying pan. Knew

where the toddler was by the cat's tail—
it followed him into the yard.

Fig tree. Stars in the ceiling
at an Italian restaurant.

She never liked her food drowned
in tomato sauce. When she wanted

to sit down on something soft,
she would go visiting across the street

or she would watch the neighbors
baste their turkey through her window.

It was like a stage play. A lot of mutton.
Finding coins with the baby in the park.

She could take the bus downtown and waltz
with these coins in her purse, completely

free from the Old Country feud in South Bend,
Indiana. It was all a game.

He was repairing ships coming in from the War.
He lost it. Discharged. Meteor showers for days.

IV.

They left Compton just before
their second baby

Before I had my babies,
Elfriede was back in California

her memory already missing
when I gave birth. Did she know

the palms? When first her mind
started going, she wrote these notes

on California, her youth.
At the end of the pages

she wrote the story
of her and her husband

helping a confused old woman find home.
An owl followed them all the way

down the sidewalks,
flying from palm to palm.

III. Map in My Palm

Water Castle   No. 3

Confused by what's been erased, I erase more.

I prayed for my lover to erase my features
in our children—for my Slavic-ness to disappear

in his island culture, to be near his real
culture—to have any culture at all.

For so long I felt filled with nothing
but melted snow; the water around me
sour as beer. I did not want any house

to own me. My first time I saw
a Klimt painting, that famed *Kiss,* stars pricked

my spine all the way to the nape of my neck, just like a cliché.

Klimt—womanizer, never married, possibly 14 children, also made
    of water,
both of us born under that miserable crab.

Green is good, warm light, Frida Kahlo wrote
And an olive shade is *leaves, sadness, science.*
The whole of Germany is this color. Kahlo also

moon-ruled, July-born, water. Her diary shows me
my allegiance to green. Her definition of olive
green is my father. When my ancestors

were as green as the water shining in the ponds of the apartment
where I go to meet my lover, where I conceived, the lake
around me was already forming.

It took ten wet seasons
for me to see us without glare or gloss.

It was the time we went to the mountain
at the navel of the Earth.

We saw the birth of neon
green, darkening to emerald.

Every day a variant: a little more blue
or yellow, always the combination new.

These were our days.
our years we keep touching each other.

He stays, stays, stays,
showing me the outline of my face.

It's okay, the sky got caught in the trees
and turned it to water:

God's hair. A green song:
our saga

emerged out of lake
to the tempo of his breathing

God in the mountain creating us:
born & born.

Now I can't un-see us:
our reflections, look close.

Stairwell into the Drum of the Earth

When you descended beneath the street
       into that smoke-womb, basement

       dancehall where I went for reggae
       beats each week to push death out

when the current from your eyes

       a contract between us hung
       in the heat of that tiny room

pulsing walls & ceiling painted black
       the shining strings of what I'd learn

you call pepper lights, on the DJ booth, one
       Jamaican flag, you dressed in black

       and on your chest, a mother-wound

       I winced. I had been going to drink the bitter syrup
       & forget the indigo that clung

       a father-wound. I wore around my wrist
       a black plastic bangle inscribed with *Love.*

       I wore a blue bolero. I wore
it in the blue of Mary, cerulean

with blue jeans & black tank,
       my face a moon against the walls

       & in the crowd my depression so white
escaping know-it-all bros & sad rock.

       I thought I could disappear myself in a corner
       of smoke, scoff at the few white

       couples who wandered in each week, skunk-drunk
       took up the whole floor, flail-danced.

They'd always leave before midnight
       before you & your friends from yard

showed up, dancing in a line, synchronized.
       A poem. This poem wasn't meant to be

about race like my denial that it could be

       about race when Danger spun records and toasted patois

into the mic I didn't know one day I'd understand it
       differently. Like my tears so naïve

       when Obama elected just before we met, his face
       an icon-saint pinned to our walls.

       Like thinking music can rattle out my self
       pity like when certain tracks blasted from the stacks

& you & the men beat the ceiling with the hearts
       of your palms, slapping in approval

       & you until the lights came on & you

taking me up to the snow-crusted dirt
    to walk with me over the earth

    & teach me how
    not to cry.

O Fortune, Are You Listening?

Having washed you down the sink
and off the plates of my children

are you swimming in the egg
and milk of my sewer?

Are you there in my cracked patio
slab humming with sparrows?

O fortune! I grow old
and the moon becomes your wheel.

I watch you by the dark
of our broken street lamps.

I am still without
kingdom. They say

you can melt
my poverty like ice.

This is what happened
when you made me

a troubled match in love
but still, still the wheel comes up,

the fog finally lifts.
After forsaking me,

I am secure. Now
I am one of those

who will pluck strings
and sing—of what is left

with what is left—
my weapons, my selves.

Lilies Falling from the Ceiling

Once, my children hung inside me
attached by veins. I imagine ribbons

twisted. More than once, my brain
reduced to ribbons, humming

all night wanting a way out.
Sometimes I stared at objects

smashing them inside my stare.
Imagined toppling the television

off its little plastic pedestal
or cracking secondhand plates

hard on soft linoleum
when toddlers wouldn't let me sleep,

the lilies stopped me like stars—
ghost-white ones I bought

from the dollar store, cut up
and hung upside down attached

by satin ribbons, falling from the ceiling.
They watched over the whole industry of us:

hustling woman with exhaustion and children
who grew and grew against

my dissatisfaction winding its way through
the apartment like a snake.

Against my panics, they learned to finally sleep,
legs lengthening every night.

What Did We Do to Each Other in Our Past Lives?

a week after conception   I felt the sphere of cells
gnaw a notch   into the dead center of me
my baby father laughed   and sang
circled his arms around me   to show

gnaw a notch   into the dead center of me
how big   my belly would get
circled his arms around me   to show
he was right   he was happy as we rode in the gold car

how big   my belly would get
our baby kicked   with each boom of bass
he was right   he was happy as we rode in the gold car
I used to laugh at his songs   until I was living it

our baby kicked   with each boom of bass
real man a gallis   so many gyals
I used to laugh at his songs   until I was living it
the joke's on you   god says   when I get to him in sleep

real man a gallis   so many gyals
I could pretend   to condense him to a raindrop
the joke's on you   god says   when I get to him in sleep
I'm still knotted   bedded down by need

I could pretend   to condense him to a raindrop
yet I don't want to worship   a husband-god
I'm still knotted   bedded down by need
I painted my walls   moon-color

yet I don't want to worship   a husband-god
my baby father laughed   and sang
I painted my walls   moon-color
at my altar needing   pails of water to anoint me

Strollers in My Throat

Pregnant again, moving back
again my lotion, my combs,
my paintings tucked in his corners.

As I dried my face in the rust-
edged mirror, the atmosphere
of the cramped bath shifted.

Maybe there was joy behind
my shoulder blade when I felt
a whoosh of cold sweep there

and in the softest moth-fur
whisper: *Elfriede,* my grandmother
with mind gone, who I hadn't seen

in years. I knew it was her goodbye
flying past my trouble, off
the earth. My father's phone call

confirmed it. I was impressed
she found me in cold Indiana—
that place of every heavy

ache in her life. As one by one
each foul memory fell from her,
finally she was sent back to her beloved

California to die oblivious of place,
of palm trees. To be turned to ash, to be
tossed into sea with rings of flowers.

It Was Mango Season

and also fly season, and rainy season
he explained that first time in Jamaica
inside his sister's house while we
swiped air, shocked flies with these
small electric stringed rackets
but no matter how many hollow
carcasses dropped, another crawled
through the wood-slatted windows.

Half-translucent ants made trails everywhere—
up stairs, walls, and streaming out
the humming microwave, unharmed.

We ate street-bought rum raisin
ice cream cones that liquefied
too fast as the afternoon drench
flattened banana tree leaves.

When adults left children refusing
to say where they're going, *soon come*
was hours. And there was no *Hello, Goodbye*.

This was as soothing as the texture of the air to me—
my perceived slights from him now seen
in context—common, familial, but so
What now?

It can never be reversed, and some love
has settled in.

The machete, quick
whispered before he struck the coconut.

He handed me half to drink
the water from its shell,
lifted the other half to the baby's lips.

Everything Is Separated by Water

after María Magdalena Campos-Pons

I didn't know I could be such a prolific fountain:
a multitude of tears for your vanity and stony distance,

a deluge of blood for bringing in our sons,
a stream of milk spouting when one of them unlatched—

it arched across the room
and reached you. Everything is separated

by water:
our homelands and our expectations

of love. I once asked you:
How did you find me in this Northern country and ruin my life?

But I meant: Why was it you who made my life?
Who saved my life?

Who, in the season of my largest loss, when I thought of nothing
but suicide, brought me my longed for

lovelies—the babies—and looked at me, not turning away,
just turning into—

one midnight you took me back to your island and you married the air.
I saw you only by your gold.

And though you lent me the motto life gave you:
Save your tears,

I was feeling generous. My old destructions—
all night I fed them to the sea.

Boy Formed by Heat

Moon thickening in a dry June
     my *wash-belly*
     son born in a season like this

Once-in-century drought now
     once in ten years

I remember the hospital window
     where my stare landed
     on the green lawn gone
     to straw

Me and my baby in the veil
     between worlds where I almost crossed
     in a river of my blood

We were wrapped in white sheets
     whispery as a cloud,
     the earth's lure muted

Slowly, we came to that summer

Our apartment garden
The callaloo wilting

My baby's father would
     make a cup with his hand
     water the plants from a bowl
     and they would rise, alive

Now our boy formed by heat
        is tall, swift as wind, placing an orb
        into the net
        little wings at his ankles

All these onlookers
        I could tell them the story
        of all our years at the edge

What we ate
        air and air
        but they wouldn't
        believe it

His long feet
        his grandmother says
        to *wash in lime* or *use*
        BLUE, to *cut the curses,*
        badmind

I finally see them
        from the hard ground

Clouds fattening

I open my mouth to them
        but the wet won't drop

I ask, *What are you bringing*
        to us this time?

When You Tell Me to Close the Gap in Our Youngest Son's Teeth, I Say No

at first because of the Morgan Parker poem
about the gap in Angela Davis's teeth speaking

to the gap in James Baldwin's smile & to all the famed
Black gap-toothed smiles & I remembered the psychic

said our Black son would be a light
would be known & how we laughed

as we walked in the park & a pack
of little girls pointed & said

There he is! There he is!
& always some child pointing, saying,

There's _____! & most importantly
when we were going down the river of grass

on a boat with your mother and she told
her regret, how she closed her gap

begotten by her mother, *who was a Maroon*
descended from the people who fought

against the white slavers & lived free
in the Blue Mountains

& if only I *coulda seen*
her mother *when she laughed, she was*

such a pretty Black woman with a gap
in her perfect teeth

& she tells me a gap means
beauty and luck and strength

her ancestor, the Maroon,
his ancestor so strong, so lucky

so she tells me,
don't close it.

Montego Bay

I ask uncle what that tree is
in the hills a neon not exactly
magenta, not orange, but brighter
than red in a lacy legume tree.
He says *Fire Tree*.
I explain to my sons
yes, there is destination
somewhere. I answer, yes,
the rag is on your father's head,
and a trip is not point to point
and a couple stops is not—
listen, a couple is not two, maybe four—
every time we touch road—
pattie, Champagne Kola,
then bag of Jamaican apple,
bouquet of mangoes in a plastic bowl.
Next, buy the refurbished tire
then go to the next place
to change the tire.
In America it's about speed
and being entertained.
Here—time expands, the heat holds
its hands. This is about endurance
and a hustle. We park by the boys on motorbikes.
Everyone's a hustler, uncle says
as he pays the boy to cut
in the hours long KFC line in Mobay.
Yes, KFC, but here the seasoning, they boast,
is different. There's some hassling
with the money and then
there's the hot bucket

in our laps in the hot van
the honking, the twisting road.
We speed back to the house
in one of Mobay's gated schemes.
We take it to the top floor
of the house that has no roof yet.
We sit on cinder and eat.
When the boys and their cousins turn over
plates with unbroken bones,
with a little meat attached,
they say these kids can't appreciate.
Uncle says I never had a piece of chicken
until age 14. I say I know when I clean
their father's plates—the bone bits,
marrow gone. Uncle says people back then
had to learn how to eat from nothing
Grandma says, Yes, but I prefer the neck.

All Inclusive Resort

the pool a flickering
turquoise fan too shallow.
rivers of chlorine run around
the gluttony: all you can eat
burger, hot dog, jerk
chicken, ice cream.
tiny cups slick with sanitizer.

nausea. travel-sick.
ceiling plaster rain
in the bathroom.
a little run down.

one bright spot:
half the guests here
are from the island we're on
and same for the rest of our
party: my partner's family
because the cost
the off-season.
and gladly, they are enjoying.
I am the dumb, numb one.

I feel off
I'd rather
be back in the sweltering
little cinder block home.
grandma's simple callaloo
and dumpling breakfast
the best meal I had all trip.

here, we all scatter
to the pool, the beach
the cold rooms
blaring rickety air conditioners
that never cease and always
someone is drunk
from the rum punch.

soon enough
we'll go back to our bodies
piled into the van:
the closeness, conversation
my nephew's little fingers
on my phone screen, playing
the word game together
and the heat: brutal friend
carving away at me.

Black River

Nine of us in the van, swaying, sticky hot.
When uncle's thermos of rum punch hits,
we're flying, come close to meeting
angels when we pass near curves.

We swerve and bump around the craters
down highway 88, then A2 along
the coast, stop in White House:
fried fish, okra soup, festival,
but I'm all stomach, clenched, bad traveler.

When we finally arrive in Black River,
driving along High Street, I get a chill
as we pass St. John's white gothic windows
chipped, and the old brown brick.
And then the scarred white colonial courthouse.
My mind flashes on those who used to worship
and rule—the ones who enslaved the ancestors
of my children's father and the family
who hum and sing in the van around me.

When we reach River Safari, the men
walk over the bridge to drink beers, and I sit
with the women and talk about love.

Staring upriver at the wharf, I don't know
until I go home that it's marked—death-spot
of the *Zong* and of the slave market where
my son's forebears might have stood.

One uncle is catching crabs in a bottle,
another is eating guava from the tree.
When my love offers me one,
I refuse, so he plucks
a hibiscus bloom, puts it behind my left ear
This will make you feel better.

Once we get in the boat, I carry it over the water
until the petals aren't strong enough
for the boat's drag of wind.

I pack it away in my bag somewhere in the middle
of the red mangroves, and a little of my sickness
lifts with the egrets. We're all laughing at uncle
and our guide Andrew in the khaki suit who
knows the facts and jokes and slaps the water
and pets the thousand-pound crocs like dogs.

Driving back, passing the not-
past-past: those structures shivering
ghostly. I note to look them up.
I grip the back of a headrest.

Grandma falls asleep against me
and all four boys in the back, cousins
shoulder to shoulder, drift off, mouths agape.

The Lovers

The water between us never drained;
it's rippling like a flag.

How many times I become a storm,
leave for my own place,

only to be back in your new rooms,
my old lover, the same pond-lake.

They say *The Lovers* means choice, maybe
the lovers we've chosen to have while still

having each other. We've stretched the water.
I've turned and run. You've chased.

Nights, my belly grew a Gemini child
as I listened to the fountain in the pool.

The lovers are fools, right?
The garlands of flowers they pick apart.

I only now see how much fruit
we've let drop and rot—

Love has always been too sweet
for either of us to stomach.

We've kept the pain with our pleasure, still
circling the water, our magnet.

Where I Have Been All These Years

Through the dark nights at Eagle Creek
Court Apartments, the circular
windows above the doorways

were little lakes of light in the brick,
little full moons beaming.

My fate kept sending me back—
my oldest son toddled the sidewalks there.

Then, pregnant with a second son, I roamed
and strollered the confines of this sculpted landscape—

its sycamore and pine, its pumped fountain and waterfall,
wishing to possess something beyond my tiny slab
of rented concrete and patch of soil.

Now the boys are tall. Now we visit. We find a clearing
at the edge of the parking lot. Now we follow the slope
down, follow the way the rain flows.

We pass a nest of pink blankets in dead leaves,
and see a pool of green glass—empty beer bottles,
but there is only the sound of water here.

When we squeeze through the ripped chain-link,
we emerge into the other world—away from the overpass,
the gravel path. We wonder at the moving creek—
now steel-gray, now dark-emerald.

I touch the illuminated map in my palm
to find out where I have been all these years,
to learn the bits of our river all around me,

the creeks that pumped their life downstream, downtown
while I grew two more hearts, while I lived
and beat my own path into the grass
and thought of the river far away and my faith in it.

I didn't even see my own hands so close to its mouth.

I Learned Love Late

an hour after moon rise
and full in my sign

>sign of the shell,
>the home, the breast

mine in your mouth
your secrets fallen out
you closed the door to them

>the others, what was before
>when our children were little and
>I was always scuttling away, disaster

used to happen and then you'd step
into a small room with me in it, shut
the door while babies and not babies
cooed, still awake

>once again, we don't wait
>for sleep, we move together
>ocean heavy, winter evening dark
>shuddering and shimmering

we made the long legged almost-teens
in the other room who watch basketball

>on TV, the moon is round
>as the ball in the net

the moon was round outside my window
the late-night, the after-going-out
when the first boy was made

        now we remake
        the room gone buzzy, downright
        thronging, what angels

allowed us to keep feeling
love, to keep arching into
each other, trying
to see, to really see each other

        I just did the math, all these years
        two thousand times your body
        became a part of my body, such

wet relief to lift for a moment
the foggy veil of this terrible
earth, two thousand gifts

        what day was it
        that I finally knew

inside my shell, my breast
you have built yourself a home

About the Author

Natalie Solmer is the founder and Editor in Chief of *The Indianapolis Review,* and is an Assistant Professor of English at Ivy Tech Community College. She grew up in South Bend, Indiana, went to Clemson University in South Carolina, and majored in horticulture. Before her return to grad school and career in teaching, she worked as a grocery store florist for 13 years. Her poetry has been published in numerous publications such as: *Colorado Review, North American Review, The Literary Review,* and *Pleiades.*

Natalie's website is:
nataliesolmer.com

www.ingramcontent.com/pod-product-compliance
Lightning Source LLC
Chambersburg PA
CBHW030053170426
43197CB00010B/1505